COSMIC
BOWLING

ESSENTIAL POETS SERIES 277

Guernica Editions Inc. acknowledges the support of
the Canada Council for the Arts and the Ontario Arts Council.
The Ontario Arts Council is an agency of the Government of Ontario.
We acknowledge the financial support of the Government of Canada.

Cornelia
Hoogland

COSMIC
BOWLING

Ted
Goodden

GUERNICA
EDITIONS

TORONTO • CHICAGO • BUFFALO • LANCASTER (U.K.)
2020

Michael Mirolla, editor
Cover and interior design: Rafael Chimicatti
Cover image: Ted Goodden
Guernica Editions Inc.
287 Templemead Drive, Hamilton (ON), Canada L8W 2W4
2250 Military Road, Tonawanda, N.Y. 14150-6000 U.S.A.
www.guernicaeditions.com

Distributors:
Independent Publishers Group (IPG)
600 North Pulaski Road, Chicago IL 60624
University of Toronto Press Distribution (UTP),
5201 Dufferin Street, Toronto (ON), Canada M3H 5T8
Gazelle Book Services, White Cross Mills
High Town, Lancaster LA1 4XS U.K.

First edition.
Printed in Canada.

Legal Deposit – Third Quarter
Library of Congress Catalog Card Number: 2019949205
Library and Archives Canada Cataloguing in Publication
Title: Cosmic bowling : the I ching poems / Cornelia Hoogland ;
[art by] Ted Goodden.
Other titles: I ching poems
Names: Hoogland, Cornelia, author. | Goodden, Ted, artist.
Series: Essential poets ; 277.
Description: Series statement: Essential poets series ; 277
Identifiers: Canadiana 20190174617 | ISBN 9781771835374 (softcover)
Classification: LCC PS8615.O5152 C67 2020 | DDC C811/.6—dc23

Contents

For Maya, Avery, Mihai, Adrian, and Stefan

1. *Ch'ien,* The Creative

Six unbroken lines forge a white-hot connection.
We're born for heat. Maybe lava, earth's
molten core; maybe the sun's energy.

We human neuro-electric light bulbs,
winking our 100 watts. The six steps equal
six dragons to climb. They are *not* sleeping.

2. *K'un,* The Receptive

Snow fills the forest framed by the ebony window.
The fairy tale queen
puts down her needlework and wishes for a child.

The season deepens. Hoarfrost numbs the grass, ice
needles the ground. Six cows
in the winter field, their hot breath steaming the air.

3. *Chun,* Difficulty at the Beginning

Like playing cards, the jelly girls flip over the lawn.
Somersault, backbend. Each fanning rib
is a ruffling wake. Each quivering heart on its high wire

over Niagara. Difficult and mysterious
to be alive? Maybe. But when you're
nine years old, easy to gamble on handsprings.

4. *Mêng*, Youthful Folly

Keep moving, don't stop. Hesitating at the crease of the net
is folly. *You're young*, says the Tao, *you don't know life
flows through you in waves*. Across the mid-day sky the moon

is sometimes visible. The red-lipped cranberry bosses the bees
from bloom to bloom; seed hitches a ride in the dog's fur. The bean
planted under the ground doesn't know, at first, which way is up.

5. *Hsü,* Waiting

Light emerges out of these sculptures.
They have their own pulse, steady and below
awareness. Not just the individual images

but the transitions among them. Nothing's fixed.
The sculptor releases beauty; it will return in another creation.
He's the accomplice, handmaiden to his work.

6. *Sung*, Conflict

Awake at three a.m. in racketing rain, drumming
run-off. Boggy demons muddy me; riddles of early hurt
and private mire. But I'm finished cringing.

My emotions are weathers, storms passing through:
saved in the flood or drowning? It's the sorting
that's soul work. At three a.m., in the dark, in the rain.

7. *Shih,* The Army

Diversity was the surprise; east-end protestors mingled
with suits on arena steps across Canada, in the cold,
in 2003. Country in a tug-of-war. Should we join

the invasion, declare war on Iraq? In hand knit,
hipster, indigenous and religious dress—our collective *NO.*
Jack Layton and hot coffee kindling our resolve.

8. *Pi,* Holding Together

Oceans call to each other. Pacific for the Atlantic, the Atlantic
for the Arctic. The Qu'Appelle river speaks the mother-tongue
of the Assiniboine, the Athabasca, the Slave. In the Gwich'in language

Canada's longest river is *Yu-kun-ah*, meaning *great river*.
Earth's magnetic fingers drag beach pebbles to its core.
Floating from the jazz club at the alley's end—piano music.

9. *Hsiao Ch'u,* The Taming Power of the Small

The power of even a small restraint
accumulates by withholding
its expression. Harder

than you might think. Swift kick
to the soccer goal takes as much force
as restraining that kick. My foot trembles.

10. *Lü,* Treading

In an effort to ground myself, I choose the adverbs—
the *how*—of being here. Unhesitatingly, the fairy tale hero
sets the trapped fox free. On his morning commute,

graffiti in oversize script on the subway wall: *Name what is
doomed to disappear. Name things done and undone.* At the beach
my flip-flops raise clouds of sand fleas that lift and hover.

11. *T'ai*, Peace

The belly's muscles reach beneath the ribcage
to the heart. Heart-music is amplified
in a hundred feet of headroom. Like looking into

the cathedral's vaulted ceiling. Green bough taps
your window, leans into your troubled night. Here comes favour,
an end to narrowness. The double gates swing wide.

12. *P'i*, Standstill

We're at the zenith. Heaven pulls back,
wind rushes the green beans, ransacks
the currant bushes. Hummingbird sails

past Sweet William's spent bloom. Dear summer,
don't leave. Red raspberry, abundant
on the cane—already my blue bowl misses you.

13. *T'ung Jên,* Fellowship with Men

In the camp they became numbers. One day, returning under guard from work, a dog met them. They called him Paddy. Paddy appeared every day at four a.m.

assembly and was waiting when they returned, wagging his tail, angling his head as he sidled toward them. Paddy never doubted they were men.

14. *Ta Yu,* Possession in Great Measure

Waiting for the ferry, I see a bird. A cedar waxwing?
Its mask—two black triangles pointing to the eyes—
is both ancient god *and* circus clown. I'm the lucky

witness of a trickster world poised in two or more
directions. The sun diamonds down, tugs
the seedlings raising their fists through dirt.

15. *Ch'ien*, Modesty

Lowliness—a quality of the earth—is the reason my garlic
patch is favoured in this poem. Each unassuming
clove reminds the bulb of its papery beginning,

a modesty that elevates the plant above the great mountain.
Likewise, sun at its zenith is a moment of fullness as well as
decline. They are the same moment.

16. *Yü,* Enthusiasm

In high summer, the most northerly gulf island—
like a *Christo* installation—is wrapped in a *Running Fence* of feeling.
The Pleiades crest the sky in a tidal radius of forty-three

light years. Luminous. Christo says it takes courage to create things
to be gone. Each warm night's a bonfire. We burn and dance
and fall asleep in jumbled heaps on our island under stars.

17. *Sui,* Following

Sun compels snake from under the rock, raises the flag iris
at the pond, and—sunflower in tow—wheels
across the sky. My senses may never align:

not the centre of the universe, our Copernican earth
is minion to the sun. I can almost understand the Aztecs
who ripped out human hearts and held them up in gratitude.

18. *Ku*, Work on What's Been Spoiled

Martha Stewart's glossy mag open on the table
answers the riddle of a cluttered life, the secret
to perfect skin. I work at being my best.

Birds at dawn speak to human need.
The silence when they go quiet is what music
tends toward. The indifferent wind.

19. *Lin,* Approach

Some things you can't approach directly. Birds, for one.
Binoculars in hand, wait. Things rushing past need to be seized
by the tail, though I'm not sure what they are. Are you

the kind of person who walks straight toward? Or do you circle
your heart's desire? I'm learning to recognize my friends
by their gait. Who approaches me now on slow, steady feet?

20. *Kuan,* Contemplation

At this height I not only see a great distance,
I am also seen. I forget that
others regard my example. *Full of trust*

they look up to him. What should I do with that?
Hey there, Raven, gazing toward the sea,
quietly containing your wild flight, your stony heart.

21. *Shih Ho,* Biting Through

My expert tongue guided gristle from mouth to plate, politely.
I resented the visiting cousin served the choice cut at meals.
The meat in this hexagram is dry-lean, old-dry, and tough.

I know this poem sounds pathetic, but its refusal to suppress
the drudgery of *getting through* is important. In the nursing home
your applesauce will be pureed—that too will take humour.

22. *Pi*, Grace

Transfixed, I watch a fire break
from the depth of earth, and blazing,
reveal and beautify the mountain. Even

as it destroys. The same with the cancer
that illuminated my friend. Every magnificence
she was becoming. To the end, resolve.

23. *Po,* Splitting Apart

Crazy week of not wanting you to stop—to talk or do
anything but what you were doing. I wanted it more
than my three years in women's studies, my mother's

admonitions, my own sense of my best self. The way it
made me feel. When we split up, I fell apart. That's me,
rounding out my fine principles, grounding my ideals.

24. *Fu,* Return

Sap ruddies the bare dogwood, the hillside turns purple.
Winter solstice points its pinhole camera toward the burgundy
horizon. One season completes, another begins.

A procession of choristers carry the candled dark.
I'm on a new journey myself, not so driven. Parts
of me I've neglected return, take on a burnished glow.

25. *Wu Wang,* Innocence

Confucius says: *He who departs from innocence, what does he*
come to? The wild in children, running dogs, in snap peas
poking through dirt. Valuable, the energy that's mine

to shape, I can't lose what belongs to me. I witnessed
a woman gray as a hospital blanket come back from oblivion:
bolting upright, she demanded coffee—double sugar, extra cream.

26. *Ta Ch'u,* The Taming Power of the Great

I'm learning to hold my own note in the presence
of other choristers. At choir practice, we walk around
singing *Tiny Bubbles* while weaving in and out

of each other's personal spaces. When the sopranos
sing *Make me feel happy, make me feel fine* to the top
of the Douglas fir, boughs begin swaying.

27. *I,* The Corners of the Mouth

The boundlessness of being human is the drift the self exists within.
Heron, unfolding the sky. The body is focused;
it bites into the apple it digests into thoughts (somehow);

a shiny sentence never before spoken. In the plant world,
leaves turn sunlight into sugar and release the oxygen that feeds us.
The artful things people make, or do, are also oxygen.

28. *Ta Kuo,* Preponderance of the Great

Daily, this feeling of the thinning earth. Violin strings
stretched to their limit. Crescendo in music: waiting
for the chords to resolve but they don't, they build

and build. The planet's idling on fumes, a kind of deadly
inertia. We go on being part of the problem. Like Atlas
bearing up the sky, a strained and daily quality. We suffer.

29. *K'an,* The Abysmal

The next time my boss loses it, I'm outta here.
What if I gained distance. The hexagram
says to begin with the one thing that's lucid, proceed

from there. Move through humiliation to speaking in a way
that creates flow. Enter the hollow between ribs of sand,
between waves that advance the tide. Or is the tide retreating?

30. *Li,* The Clinging, Fire

Pacific storms strip sand from beaches, expose a shore
of carved, conglomerate shelves. High rises and city sidewalks
are built upon the compacting weight of shell middens,

and plumes of hot, buoyant rock rising from earth's molten core.
Semis roll down the 401 alongside green fields, cows grazing.
The day I got out of my car to be near them, inhale their Jersey breath.

31. *Hsien,* Influence

Before the heart commands, the toes are flexed to run. What is
more persuasive than the heart's desires? A graceless child, dumb,
by which I mean speechless, without vocabulary—I was the

vibrating air around the bell when it stopped ringing. Running through
the cow fields, my inner sense extended beyond my body's frame.
The bright, cold universe goes on, stars the heat that bend it.

32. *Hêng,* Duration

Every 76 years, Halley's comet loops into earth's orbit,
then begins its elliptical return to the sun. In the *Divine Comedy,*
Dante says the planets are held in orbits by love.

Newton called it gravity, a balanced attraction
among moving bodies. Breath measures duration
in humans, and love binds. My arm circles my planet.

33. *Tun,* Retreat

If ears took out their earbuds; if arms' reach was toward others
rather than second helpings; if spine, like willow, bent;
if heart steadied itself; would these adjustments suffice?

Returning from the metro on the icy sidewalk, I keep
my hands out of my pockets in case I fall.
Sudden warmth where your arm steadies mine.

34. *Ta Chuang,* The Power of the Great

In this sculpture, the eye is compelled upward
though the torso, the raised arm, the head.
The pose, however, is performed on average feet,

shoe size 11, B width, on legs just long enough.
This is what power looks like: one long arc from earth
to fingertip. You climb the ladder from the ground up.

35. *Chin,* Progress

In her dusty web, her midden of carcasses—dried bits of bug,
a shelled abdomen—a spider sits, motionless except for
a twitch, nearly invisible. Something arrives, it always does.

Her legs tremble the web like Clotho at her loom,
treadle a furious wrapping motion. Nourishment
lands unbidden in the spider's net. She waits for it.

36. *Ming I,* Darkening of the Light

Let's say there are ten pictures. In nine of them
I'm what everybody thinks I am, dutiful. But in the tenth,
I'm as I know myself to be. Even when I was a kid

there was a room at my centre—it had windows
that opened to the stars. Time and space
whirled outward, except it was me expanding.

37. *Chia Jên,* The Family

If it's about the survival of the human species, if
we're to raise our kids to breeding age then wither
and slide toward death ourselves, why elaborate

a neckline with Belgian lace, why wedding dress?
And why, dear world, this ostentatious
avian eye, one yellow blink and the bird's gone?

38. *K'uei,* Opposition

I have a dog. He runs away. My practice is to exercise him
twice a day—but his? He sneaks under the fence
and returns with a rotting carcass. Such species-difference

can't be reconciled, but when we walk the beach—
when he thrusts his chest into the waves—
his spine undulating with each leap—oh, the wild in me.

39. *Chien,* Obstruction

Trekking B.C.'s coastal mountains with your mother,
obstruction is inevitable. Do you have to be Taoist
to learn adversity's value? The cougar

pulls back before leaping. *Reculer pour mieux sauter.*
In houses with cats and windowsills, people daily witness
this drawing-back, this energy-gathering moment.

40. *Hsieh,* Deliverance

Thunderstorm clears the air in one terrifying clap.
Babies sail naked and wet out of the birth canal, cry
loudly when cold air smacks their sudden lungs.

Refugees vacate the premises only when forced into exile.
Deliverance is a word understood in retrospect—though
dust clings to the throat, rubble to the breathing.

41. *Sun,* Decrease

The pandemic, when it hit, alarmed everyone everywhere.
The loudest amongst us clamoured to be vindicated,
better understood. But as a species, we sensed

we'd arrived at the beginning of awareness.
I polished my shoes for the first time in ten years while
listening to Beethoven online. What kind of virus is that?

42. *I*, Increase

A kid with a spoon bangs the table. *More!* The Tao says
change begins by observing how thunder and wind strengthen
each other. I've no idea how thunder and wind strengthen

each other. But I know hands, infant skin, the mouth's work
when my baby nursed. Pulled by a celestial tide:
my body's need to make milk, my baby's need calling milk forth.

43. *Kuai,* Breakthrough

I've always kept the day world and death
apart. Now, in near darkness and close
to Hallowe'en, the day's permeated

with you who've died. Like animal tracks
in snow, you evoke your own absence, you speak
to me. You break through, or I do.

44. *Kou,* Coming to Meet

Earth and wind in tango. Ribald August brushes
my jacket as it glides by. Just when I think
the dog days are over, summer's gypsy eyes catch

mine. I'm definitely interested, but I suspect
treachery. The vinegar apples, composting, a sour
smell below the tree. Dark, spreading bruises.

45. *Ts'ui,* Gathering Together

Union Station, Yonge at Front, rush hour. *You see that line*
moving through the station, I told you, I was one of those. Leonard Cohen
is going to war but we who live in the 905 want to get home,

pull out the lasagna, the remote control. What if we were bees,
subordinate to a hive and a queen, and we gathered nectar,
and we turned our lives into honey. Sweetened our rivers. The air.

46. *Shêng,* Pushing Upward

Success is assured. I'm trying to work differently, write
in the confidence of success. Visualize my ragged lines already
in the hands of a reader, just a matter of me catching up.

Or the tagged Monarch butterfly, powered by nectar and instinct,
at rest in Belo Horizonte, its 3000-kilometre flight complete.
Hard work, but who would Sisyphus be without his rock.

47. *K'un,* Oppression

I stake my life on what I believe. Maybe I'm going crazy,
but in that craziness is something to claim.
Huck Finn—on the raft with Jim—refused to turn in

his friend. Huck knew full-well he'd go to hell
for defying the law. Rough water below, but I stand tall as possible,
hoist my inadequate self to my shoulder. Lift my eyes.

48. *Ching,* The Well

The image derives from the pole-and-bucket well
of ancient China. Here the Tao describes itself,
the way the seeker lowers her bucket into the depths

of her own reservoir, awakens. So much space inside us.
Can we lower ourselves, risk what Rilke calls a second,
larger life inside? Trust the rope descends to water.

49. *Ko,* Revolution

My first miracle was the Monarch butterfly; the way she looked
around Miss Mitten's grade two classroom, climbed her twig
in the aquarium, arced her slow, wet wings, charged them

with flight. More marvellous than Clark Kent squeezing into
the telephone booth, morphing into Superman. And what, by the way,
did he do with his shoes, his suit, his black-rimmed glasses?

50. *Ting,* The Cauldron

Here's a situation: an artist creates a significant work, furthers
her culture. But even six-line poems must find their audience.
On stage, the artist overcomes nervousness by serving the work.

She enters each phrase, the rocky shore-line they pebble. The
sandstone shelf. Always the possibility of a surge channel, a crevasse
gorged with crashing waves funnelling energetically upward.

51. *Chên*, The Arousing

For seven years you'll lose your treasure, you'll climb
the nine hills. This is not a case of a single
shock but of repeated shocks with no breathing space

between. Tear the calendar off the wall, load
your gear and tackle, hurl your Chevy down the road—
to the secret pool, the swimming fish.

52. *Kên,* Keeping Still, Mountain

How to achieve a quiet heart. Always two directions,
always two things and the balance between them.
Yoga is like that. I'm on my back, pushing

the heel of my raised leg skyward as I deepen
my belly toward my spine. Centring the weight
at the core calms the nattering ego and its Twitter feed.

53. *Chien,* Development

Wolves fish the river for salmon they carry to their dens.
They feed the brains to their pups, leave the rest
for the decomposers working the forest floor.

Rain drives the nutrients to the roots of the giant trees.
When the wild goose flies to the top of the Douglas fir,
we collect its feathers for the sacred dance.

54. *Kuei Mei,* The Marrying Maiden

Very Chinese, this hexagram. Hard for westerners
to understand. How to present myself, curb
my inclination to shine, get a *leg up* in the hierarchy.

Wrong turns may be taken. *Will* be taken.
If we could see our lives from their endings. I turn
to my elders, the old ones, already there.

55. *Fêng,* Abundance

The first time my baby slid on her bum away from me
toward the world, I scooped her back into my arms.
She howled, arced her spine skyward. Scarcity is the kingdom

where people take from a sense of lack, the opposite
of the backpacker in the bus terminal I see is okay with empty arms.
Annie Dillard says time is ample, its passage sweet.

56. *Lu,* The Wanderer

Not a choice. A father puts his baby in a boat because
the city's on fire and its people have swarmed. It's tricky.
Can you trust the trafficker, who, for an outrageous fee,

says he'll run you across the water into the right port of entry?
Crouch, keep a low profile, pray the round parts of your life
survive days stuffed in this miserable hold, reeking of diesel.

57. *Sun,* The Gentle

When I was born, I was a ball of energy.
At two years old, nimble. All I beheld was Christmas
in a store window. One day my parents

had different ideas. *Why can't you behave? Be good.*
I began stuffing parts of myself into a ball. The time
my teacher shamed me, or my friend lied, or I did.

58. *Tui,* The Joyous, Lake

Graham Lake. From the dock, I swim far as
the bullrushes, joyously call to the dog, *Jump in!*
If hearts are won by the power of joy, I'll fall again

and again into the lake's wet embrace.
It likes me. Inspiration likes me, my art likes me,
my downward dog. Even my ball rushes to greet me.

59. *Huan,* Dispersion

How then should we live? Here's what the yogi knows:
his practice pauses him. Ego's high on helium—it's just that,
within poses, he lets go what's expendable. Emerging

out of daily clamour, a small voice. A summons. Maybe a loon.
This far from the Salish sea, he strains to hear. Loon makes the watery
sound that entropy makes: frozen to liquid to vapour to rain.

60. *Chieh,* Limitation

Water flows down rather than uphill. Limitations—natural laws
or self-imposed—create energy; are indispensable in the regulation
of world governments, heaven help us. But can limitations stunt?

Too long plugged into my oversized screen, I've lost
wind's circuitry, the signalling trees, this combustible wasp
fused at the waist, moving mouthparts slurping rainwater.

61. *Chung Fu,* Inner Truth

We were speaking over the phone. Your words were filaments,
the field outside my house a milky way. Phrases like flung seed,
lit stars in the prickling grass. I dreamed a democracy

in which flowering meadows commanded political will. Plants
were invited to speak their minds and hedge-fund managers tuned
their ears to grasshoppers, horseflies, the whiney No-See-Ums.

62. *Hsiao Kuo,* Preponderance of the Small

The cricket sings in the height of summer, at happy hour.
Drinks all round, then *husha husha*. This low down,
I may as well pick slugs off the lettuce. Raven doesn't surpass

herself by flying into the sun, she descends to where
her nest is. Flies down past the earth, making throaty,
knocking vocalizations. I eat my bowl of rice.

63. *Chi Chi,* After Completion

Don't throw yourself away on the world, but wait.
I meet myself every day in these hexagrams.
My impatience, my striving. I wake early and write in bed.

My sleeping partner, my dog. More and more I feel
ripples of tenderness toward me and my efforts to find balance.
Like learning to bowl. All those gutter balls.

64. *Wei Chi,* Before Completion

At birth we're turned loose into a moving field.
Endless adjustments as we position and reposition
ourselves, like geese in erratic flight

seeking permission to land. The desire to belong,
this flock-movement that so engages. The line drive, when it comes
at you, hard. The *thwack* when it hits your glove.

The *I Ching*: It Works If You Work It

AFTER FIFTY YEARS of consulting the *I Ching*, I'm still amazed that the random act of tossing three coins six times can result in a hexagram that seems anything but random in the way it speaks to my condition. A hexagram is a pattern formed by six broken and unbroken lines, resembling a horizontal barcode; each hexagram is titled and accompanied by a text. The book contains 64 hexagrams, each representing an archetypal human situation. I find it comforting to think that my personal concerns are not unique, that they can be situated within this finite world. Sometimes the hexagram speaks directly to the question I've posed and sometimes it speaks indirectly, reframing the question or bringing attention to blind spots in my outlook. In the first case, the "aha!" response is immediate; in the second, it may take several re-readings and a period of reflection, and "aha," may arrive without an exclamation point. In either case, the commentary on the hexagram brings depth to my concern and situates it within the larger cycles of the natural and the social worlds, while clothing it in fresh imagery.

My usual practice is to cast a hexagram at the solstice or equinox points of the year; sometimes I consult the *I Ching* in response to a sudden shift in circumstances that leaves me feeling anxious and uncertain about how to proceed. Thousands of years ago Hippocrates described this feeling of existential collapse: "Life is short and art long, the occasion instant, experiment perilous, decision difficult." Lately I find that "the

Hippocratic moment" arrives with the regularity of the news cycle, which daily releases a flood of despair and anxiety, not to mention fear and loathing, leaving in its wake a defeated feeling that it's too late in the game to be making the case for an ancient Chinese wisdom book. But this is exactly what I intend to do, taking heart from the *I Ching's* oft-repeated encouragement, "perseverance furthers," and seeing in the on-going unravelling of the world an opportunity for exploring an alternate worldview. I consult the *I Ching* in order to illuminate the present moment rather than forecast some predetermined future, and I find that whether I use the *I Ching* ritually, at the turn of the seasons, or more urgently in a crisis, the result is (almost) always a hexagram that addresses me personally in an uncanny way that feels like magic. I want to understand how that magic works.

Hippocrates is better known for his exhortation to the medical profession: "above all, do no harm," and this advice is consonant with the *I Ching's* tendency to privilege self-reflection over action. As Carl Jung notes in his introductory essay to the Wilhelm/Baynes edition of the book: "Even to the most biased eye it is obvious that this book represents one long admonition to careful scrutiny of one's character, attitude, and motive." Jung speaks about the role that chance plays in our lives, about the limitations of the scientific method in general, and its reliance on a narrow understanding of causality in particular. As an alternative to causality, and as a way of understanding how the *I Ching* might operate as an oracle, Jung proposes the concept of "synchronicity," which he defines as, "taking the events in space and time as meaning something more than mere chance, a peculiar interdependence of objective events among themselves as well as with subjective (psychic) states of the observer or observers." I appreciate Jung's attempt to build a bridge between Eastern and Western worldviews, but I wonder if his concept is anything more than mysticism dressed up in pseudo-scientific language. It's only towards the end of the essay that Jung addresses the elephant in the room:

> On the other hand, any person of clever and versatile mind can turn the whole thing around and show how I have projected my subjective contents into the symbolism of the hexagrams. Such a critique, though catastrophic from the standpoint of Western rationality, does no harm to the function of the *I Ching*. On the contrary, the Chinese sage would smilingly tell me: "Don't you see how useful the *I Ching* is in making you project your hitherto unrealized thoughts into its abstruse symbolism?"

I'm relieved when Jung finally mentions that projection might be at work, and inclined to ask, "what else could it possibly be?" Jung suggests that consulting the *I Ching* is like visiting the land of Oz, and that the wizard behind the curtain is yourself, disguised as a Chinese sage. Speaking from my own experience as a clinical psychologist, the *I Ching* has two essential qualities which underlie its effectiveness as a universal projection screen: otherness and openness. The "otherness" comes from the book's origin in a time and place so far removed from ours that it allows Western readers to project their imaginations freely, unburdened by familiar assumptions. This otherness also applies in contemporary China, whose people have the same distant relationship to the *I Ching* that present-day Greeks have to the Parthenon.

The second quality of "openness" is derived from the disparate philosophies of Laotse and Confucius, who laid down the woof and the warp of the text in an open-weave, their irreconcilable differences combining, or more to the point, not combining, to create a spacious text, an open invitation to the psychic ventriloquism that allows your wise self to speak through metaphor to your anxious self. But it was the lesser-known figure of King Wen who created the loom these contrasting threads were woven upon.

The *I Ching* is a palimpsest of Buddhist, Confucian and Taoist influences. I like to think of it as a thoroughly composted text, laid down in layers. The text has three founding fathers whose contributions correspond to the traditional division of the hexagram into three realms, each realm consisting of two lines. At the bottom, King Wen represents the realm of earth (the natural); in the middle, Confucius outlines the realm of man (the cultural); Laotse occupies the two lines at the top, the realm of heaven (the spiritual). The transformation of a pre-existing oracle into a humanistic text began three millennia ago with King Wen; five hundred years later the *I Ching* was enriched by the contributions of Confucius, born in 551 BCE, and Laotse, born twenty years later. Though contemporaries, these two held wildly divergent philosophies; Laotse once chided Confucius about "all this huffing and puffing, as though you were carrying a big drum and searching for a lost child."

KING WEN: SOMETIMES
THERE IS NOTHING YOU CAN DO

King Wen's contribution is foundational and lies at the bottom of the compost heap. He is a semi-historical, semi-mythological figure, and scholarly debate continues about where to place the dividing line. There is general agreement however that the *I Ching* existed in a rudimentary form before King Wen's time, perhaps as long as a thousand years before. The *I Ching* that King Wen inherited, so to speak, was a binary-based fortune telling system of 64 patterns, probably derived from the practice of scapulimancy, which is to say, it was a bone oracle used to foretell the outcomes of perennial human interests of love, war and the harvest.

King Wen was the founder of the Chou Dynasty before he was taken captive by the tyrant Chou Hsin. Like Nelson Mandela, he put his prison time to good use by studying the oracle. His personal history gave him a rare understanding of both power and powerlessness and this experience informed the meaning he read into the patterns. King Wen wrote a text to accompany each of the hexagrams, a labour completed by his son, the Duke of Chou. This is the transformative moment in the evolution of the *I Ching,* comparable to the Golden Age of Greek sculpture, when dynamic movement animated previously static and ceremonial sculptural forms.

King Wen's writings, presented as "judgements," created a critical space for the entry of free will, allowing that human agency could shape one's fate and fortune. The 29th hexagram for example, represents an abyss, but after King Wen, it's no longer a foregone conclusion that you are fated to fall into it. King Wen introduces the possibility that one could see the danger and use it as an opportunity to pause, to reflect, and to refine one's character, for character is developed through the effort to understand one's circumstances and to act accordingly. King Wen was all about character refinement, but his precarious political situation informed his judgments, which emanate from a sense of caution. His commentaries are concerned with achieving success whenever possible but above all, they are concerned with remaining beyond reproach. The reader often encounters the words, "No blame" in the judgements: that's King Wen's voice, speaking to us from three thousand years ago.

CONFUCIUS: IT'S NOT ALL ABOUT YOU

Confucius lived in chaotic times, which might account for the emphasis he placed upon order and social harmony. He is best understood as a reformer and an upholder of family values (patriarchal family values, I acknowledge). He felt that human relationships needed to follow clear outlines of duty, culture and reason, and he believed that ritual observances could reconcile individual desires to the needs of family, community, and government. "A virtuous leader," he said, "is like the wind: the moral character of those beneath him is the grass. When the wind blows, the grass bends." Confucius died convinced that he was a failure, but his teachings were collected by his disciples and recorded in *The Analects of Confucius*.

Several centuries after his death, by imperial decree in 136 B.C.E., Confucianism became the official religion in China for two millennia. Government officials espoused the teachings of Confucius; poets and writers favoured Laotse (and Chuang-tse, his main disciple). When those writers and poets became officials themselves, they endorsed Confucius openly and read Laotse secretly. You can still discern Confucius's voice in the commentaries of the *I Ching*, huffing and puffing, pointing to the path of social harmony and order. But Confucius was not only a moralist; many of his sayings are both pithy and substantial: "By three ways do we learn: first by reflection, which is the noblest; second by imitation, which is the easiest; third by experience, which is the bitterest."

LAOTSE: THIS TOO WILL PASS

Laotse, the founding father of Taoism, speaks intuitively, through natural imagery, in the voice of the mystic. The temperaments of Laotse and Confucius are over-simplified when presented as a yin/yang contrast, but Laotse does lean to the yin side. The familiar symbol of the Tao (*The Way*) visually summarizes the philosophy of Taoism: the dialectic interplay of polar opposites, dark and light, yin and yang in perpetual motion (each containing the seed of its opposite) represents a doctrine of universal reversion to eternal cycles, where every end becomes a new beginning. Life is always in flux and change is the only constant; growth alternates with decay like night with day; attaining the prime of one's strength marks the beginning of decline. From this worldview it follows that we should move through life without striving, as water flows around obstacles, and not struggle for self-advantage. Laotse often taught through paradox, emphasizing for example, the strength expressed through apparent weakness. The Tao is a path that requires humility and gentleness—qualities reflected in other spiritual traditions, such as Christ's *Sermon on the Mount*, where the teaching is similarly clothed in paradox.

The philosophies of all three foundational figures go against the grain of dominant Western values, which is a very good reason for considering them now. King Wen's hard–earned wisdom—that you can't control your circumstances, but you can control the way you respond to circumstances—goes against our preference for action over contemplation. "Just do it," is a corporate motto that reflects our widespread cultural bias for "doing" something, it hardly matters what. Better yet, do several things at once—multi-task! King Wen's advice is more in line with the Zen masters: "Don't just do something—sit there!"

Confucius' emphasis upon serving the needs of the family and the larger community can be seen as a corrective to our increasing focus on the individual. Hyper–individualism no doubt serves the corporate agenda—the self–actualizing individual requires a lot of gear—but elevating the individual to such heights undermines social cohesion and carries a cost, paid for in the coin of widespread alienation and plain old loneliness.

The influence of Laotse on the text is profound; indeed, the *I Ching* can be read as a handbook for applying Taoism to daily life. Taoism challenges the very idea of "progress;" a basic premise of western culture that seems to float like a cork upon the turbulent waters of human history. This idea is so foundational that it goes unnoticed, like the phrase "moving forward," used routinely as filler in political discourse and containing the unspoken assumption that we all know and can agree which direction "forward" is, and that it's not over the edge of the cliff. However, the Intergovernmental Panel on Climate Change sees that cliff coming into view within a decade if we continue moving forward. Since a linear understanding of progress has brought us to this precipice, it's at least possible that a Taoist paradigm of cyclical change might serve us better at this moment. Laotse understood that living systems do not move forward for long without moving backwards again and that continuous growth is unbalanced, a symptom of disease.

A cartoon appeared in the *New Yorker* when I was an undergraduate student in clinical psychology. The cartoon showed a male artist painting a female nude; the model was obese, the artist, morbidly thin, and the painting on his easel depicted a woman with the body of a Playboy pin-up. This cartoon suggested an essential truth about how projection distorts our perception of reality: projection was unconscious, subjective and bad; perception was conscious, objective and good; and reality was Reality—nothing virtual about it. To my mind these three nouns—perception, projection and reality—occupied three corners of a triangle that could be subject to trigonometric measurement and therefore to correction by deploying the instruments in the clinical psychologist's toolbox. I found this cartoon image motivational at the time and when I think of it now, I realize it's not so far removed from the popular understanding of projection. Nonetheless, it's a doltish template to lay upon something as subtle as the interface between the mind and the world.

Besides over-estimating the clinical psychologist's tools, which are notional, this image has two other shortcomings. One is philosophical and the other might be called political. First, it reifies abstract concepts which, considered on their own, are epistemologically wobbly; projection, perception and reality are mutually interdependent for any claim to meaning, and those meanings are contested. Secondly, it considers the individual in isolation from the world, which is more than naïve—it's a serious distortion of human life. I've come to see that the hard-edged triangle representing the individual needs to be swapped out for the image of a little bubble with a semi-permeable membrane, floating in the ocean of its surrounding culture.

In the collective world, clinical psychologists serve as foot soldiers who patrol the disputed borders of the normal curve and sort people according to standard deviations from this curve. But being "normal" is hardly an aspirational goal, it's only a measure of how well an individual has absorbed the dominant cultural values. After a few tours of duty most clinical psychologists experience the futility of treating individuals in isolation of their social setting and begin to suspect that Abraham Maslow was on to something when he coined the phrase, "the psychopathology of the normal." So, what are we actually talking about when we talk about projection? Clearly, trigonometry does not apply.

What I most admire about Jung's essay is the way he poses questions to the *I Ching*, allowing the book to speak for itself.

Long practised in dream analysis, Jung interprets the hexagrams offered in response to his questions, creating a dialogue with the book. Following his example, I asked the *I Ching* a basic question on behalf of the unravelling world, "What should we do now"? In response I received the 18th hexagram, "Work on What Has Been Spoiled." I would encourage everyone to read this hexagram in full, but here is a brief summary. We are living in a state of decay (decadence), in which "gentle indifference" is overlaid with "rigid inertia," and where the result is stagnation. "Since this implies guilt, the conditions embody a demand for removal of the cause." The 18th hexagram however is not dismal in its outlook: "What has been spoiled through man's fault can be made good again through man's work." "It is not immutable fate that has caused this state of corruption, but rather the abuse of human freedom." The entire hexagram turns on this last phrase, on the need to identify "the abuse of human freedom."

Being a slow thinker, I thought for a long time about the yin-yang relationship of freedom and responsibility before I came to the realization that "limited liability"—the legal status which gives corporate entities the same standing as individual persons under the law—might well qualify as an "abuse of human freedom." Limited liability gives licence to multinational corporations to exploit the natural and human resources of the planet, and to privatise their profits while socializing the damage left behind. This thought occurred to me as I was walking along the beach with my dog and it felt like an epiphany, but that's beside the point. It was a striking demonstration of the remark that Jung puts in the mouth of a Chinese sage:

"Don't you see how useful the *I Ching* is in making you project your hitherto unrealized thoughts into its abstruse symbolism?"

It seems that by proposing the concept of projection as an explanation for how the *I Ching* works, I've only substituted one mystery for another. Even within the circumscribed field of clinical psychology, projective tests have been largely discarded, opening up space for phenomenologists such as Eva Simms, who says: "perception is never neutral but shot through with memory and desire: memory of past perceptions and desire for connecting the future with the past." There is no attention without intention, however unconscious that intention might be. I find it touching that Simms highlights our "desire to connect the future with the past." How much of our personal and collective behaviour is underwritten by the human need for continuity?

Phenomenology is based upon observation and it begins with Heidegger's precept that "we are thrown into this world." We are not detached, God-like observers but part of the universe we wish to observe. Physics has known this truth for a century. Heisenberg's "principle of uncertainty" is Taoism at the subatomic level, demonstrating that reality does not consist of solid external objects but is rather an evolving project that involves human consciousness. Some kind of quantum entanglement of the inner and outer worlds is at play, and this leads me to concede that even Carl Jung's idea of synchronicity might apply. I'm giving up a lot of ground here, but then I staked out too much to begin with and I seem to have travelled in a circle around the abiding mystery of consciousness. We can't pull back the curtain on consciousness because consciousness is the curtain itself. Max Planck, the father of quantum physics, is clear on this point: "I regard matter as derivative from consciousness. We cannot get behind consciousness. Everything that we talk about, everything that we regard as existing, postulates consciousness."

It's humbling to accept that there is something irreducibly mysterious about human consciousness, and that's probably the best attitude to take toward the *I Ching*—one of humility. Notably, the words human, humus and humility share a common root. And if there's any magic involved in the *I Ching*, that might be because the world is full of magic—you needn't look beyond the compost heap to find it. Who can really understand how potato peelings combine to form the soil that grows more potatoes, or how those potatoes, when we eat them, become a thought—even "a hitherto unrealized thought?"

When you think about it, it's miraculous that we can still recognize the wisdom of this ancient book. It suggests the possibility that we might know more than we know that we know. One could attach hope to this possibility.

Ted Goodden

Notes

Poem "16. *Yu,* Enthusiasm" refers to the artist Christo's *wrap-ping* project—the massive *Running Fence* through Northern California scrubland, in 1976. www.christojeanneclaude.net

Poem "35. *Chin,* Progress" refers to Clotho, one of the three Greek Fates in ancient mythology: Lachesis, Clotho and Atropos.

Titles and references in "The *I Ching*: It Works If You Work It" are from Richard Wilhelm and Cary F. Baynes translation of the *I Ching: Or, Book of Changes.* 3rd edition, Bollingen Series XIX. Princeton NJ: Princeton University Press, 1967, 1st edition 1950.

Simms, Eva M. 2008. *The child in the world: Embodiment, time, and language in early childhood.* Detroit, Michigan: Wayne State University Press.

Four galleries hosted the sculptures and poems of "Cosmic Bowling," under different titles. "Preponderance of the Small" showed at Articulate Ground curated by Rachelle Chinnery at the Hornby Festival, July 29-August 9, 2016.

"Book of Changes" showed at the Denman Island Art Gallery, curated Andrew Fyson, August 18-August 30, 2016.

"The Book of Changes, Notes and Gestures" showed at the Hornby Island Art Gallery in 2017.

"The Book of Changes, Notes and Gestures" showed at the Comox Valley Art Gallery, curated by Angela Somerset and Denise Lawson, June-August, 2017. www.comoxvalleyart-gallery.com/events/image-text-image-opening-events/

Alun Macanulty of Courtenay, B.C., photographed Ted Goodden's sculptures at "The Book of Changes, Notes and Gestures" exhibition at the Comox Valley Art Gallery in Courtenay, British Columbia.

Acknowledgements

Thank you to the B.C. Arts Council, the Hornby Island Arts Council and the Canada Council for the Arts for acknowledging the value of our work through financial support. Thank you to the Galleries who presented our work to the public, and to the funding bodies (League of Canadian Poets and Writers' Union of Canada), for helping bring these poems and images to audiences.

A selection of poems titled *Mammalian Heart* appeared in Arc, spring 2020, in a slightly different format. Ten poems, titled *10 Hexagrams for 10 Provinces, 3 Territories,* was a finalist for the "Canada 150 Poetry" Calgary Spoken Word Society | Single Onion | Free Fall Magazine & Canada 150 in Calgary AB.

Thank you to the wonderful people at Guernica—first and foremost, Michael Mirolla, also Rafael Chimicatti, Anna van Valkenburg, Connie McParland and Dylan Curran. Thank you, Traci Skuce, for your intelligent eye and ear in editing this manuscript. Cornelia thanks her Hornby Island writing group. Ted thanks Heinz Laffin for firing the sculptures in his pottery kiln. Special thanks to Alun Macanulty of Courtenay, B.C., for the professional photography. Thank you to the brilliant Angela Somerset and Denise Lawson of the Comox Valley Art Gallery for the quality of their curatorial attention, and to the many people who viewed the gallery shows of the poems and sculptures.

We two artists work in the context of many generations of artists whose practice has shaped life on Hornby Island in the Salish Sea. Thank you to the island itself for giving us the space and solitude necessary for this extended collaboration. We gratefully acknowledge the Puntledge and K'omox peoples on whose unceded territory we work and live.

Book of Changes: Notes and Gestures at the Comox Valley Art Gallery, Courtenay, British Columbia, June 2017

About the Artists

Cornelia Hoogland's previous seven books of poetry have been shortlisted for major prizes, and her poems are published internationally. Professor emeritus at Western (UWO), Hoogland is the founder and past Artistic Director of "Poetry London," and now, of "Poetry* Hornby Island." www.corneliahoogland.com

Ted Goodden, a visual artist working primarily in stained glass, is also a sculptor and mixed media artist. His work hangs in public and private collections, and his stained glass creations are shown in solo and group shows internationally. www.ted-goodden.net